The Urbana Free Library

To renew: call 217-367-4057
or go to "*urbanafreelibrary.org*"
and select "Renew/Request Items"

DANDY
Decimals

Lisa Arias

rourkeeducationalmedia.com

Scan for Related Titles
and Teacher Resources

Before Reading:

Building Academic Vocabulary and Background Knowledge

Before reading a book, it is important to tap into what your child or students already know about the topic. This will help them develop their vocabulary, increase their reading comprehension, and make connections across the curriculum.

1. *Look at the cover of the book. What will this book be about?*
2. *What do you already know about the topic?*
3. *Let's study the Table of Contents. What will you learn about in the book's chapters?*
4. *What would you like to learn about this topic? Do you think you might learn about it from this book? Why or why not?*
5. *Use a reading journal to write about your knowledge of this topic. Record what you already know about the topic and what you hope to learn about the topic.*
6. *Read the book.*
7. *In your reading journal, record what you learned about the topic and your response to the book.*
8. *Complete the activities at the end of the book.*

Content Area Vocabulary
Read the list. What do these words mean?

annex
decimal
denominator
equivalent
factor
fraction
numerator
scale
simplest form

After Reading:

Comprehension and Extension Activity

After reading the book, work on the following questions with your child or students in order to check their level of reading comprehension and content mastery.

1. *Explain how models help you better understand fractions and decimals. (Summarize)*
2. *How can fractions be equivalent if they have different numerators and denominators? (Asking questions)*
3. *How does money relate to decimals? (Text to self connection)*
4. *Explain how decimals show part of a whole. (Summarize)*
5. *What is the denominators purpose in the fraction? (Summarize)*

Extension Activity

Now, you be the teacher! Teach you parents, siblings, or friends how decimals or fractions can be compared. Remember strategies from the book that helped you, like the pictures. Create sample problems to have them solve. How did they do? Do they understand fractions and decimals?

TABLE OF CONTENTS

DECIMALS AND FRACTIONS

Today is going to be great
to learn how fractions and decimals relate.
As you can see,
fractions count equal parts of a whole perfectly.

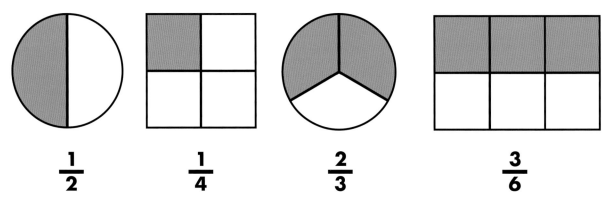

$$\frac{1}{2} \qquad \frac{1}{4} \qquad \frac{2}{3} \qquad \frac{3}{6}$$

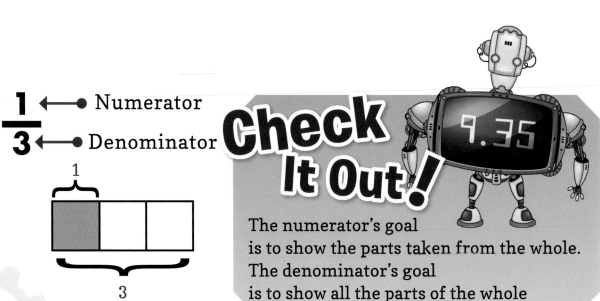

$\dfrac{1}{3}$ ← Numerator
← Denominator

Check It Out!

9.35

The numerator's goal
is to show the parts taken from the whole.
The denominator's goal
is to show all the parts of the whole

Decimals also show part of a whole. They are always based on tens, so their denominators never have to be written.

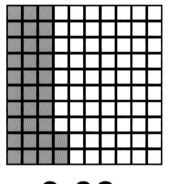

0.32

thirty-two hundredths

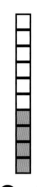

0.4

four tenths

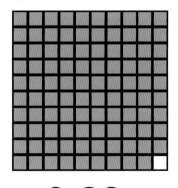

0.99

ninety-nine hundredths

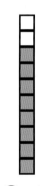

0.8

eight tenths

How to read a **decimal**:
First: Say the number you see after the decimal point.
Next: Count the number of digits after the decimal point.
If there is one digit say, "tenths."
If there are two digits say, "hundredths."

EQUIVALENT FRACTIONS

How can it be?
Fractions look different, but can be thought of equally.
Models help you clearly see a fraction's equivalency.

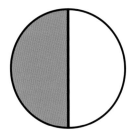 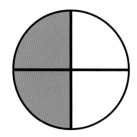 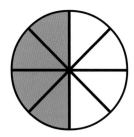

$\frac{1}{2}$ equals $\frac{2}{4}$ and also equals $\frac{4}{8}$

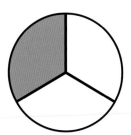 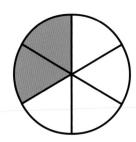 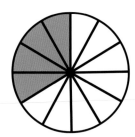

$\frac{1}{3}$ equals $\frac{2}{6}$ and also equals $\frac{4}{12}$

It doesn't matter how many parts. Fractions are **equivalent** as long as the shaded parts of an identical whole remain equal.

Name and explain which **fraction** in each set is NOT equivalent.

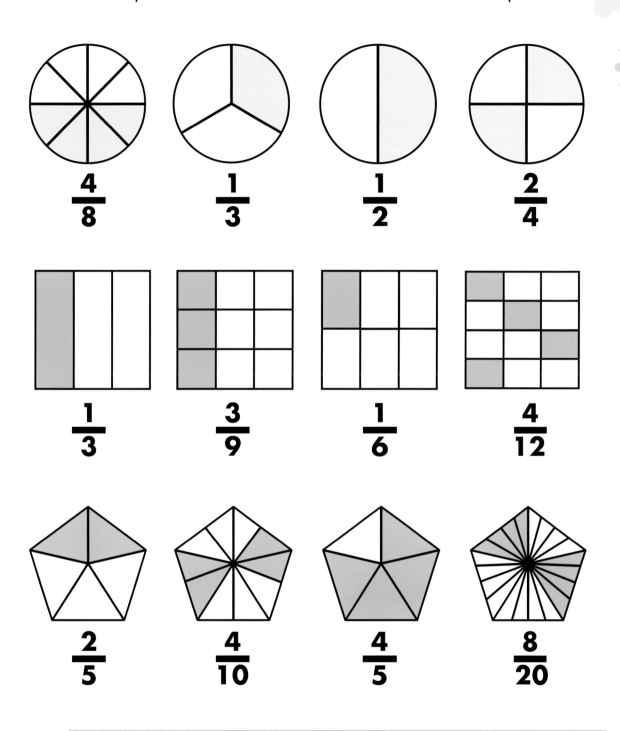

$$\frac{4}{8} \qquad \frac{1}{3} \qquad \frac{1}{2} \qquad \frac{2}{4}$$

$$\frac{1}{3} \qquad \frac{3}{9} \qquad \frac{1}{6} \qquad \frac{4}{12}$$

$$\frac{2}{5} \qquad \frac{4}{10} \qquad \frac{4}{5} \qquad \frac{8}{20}$$

Scaling

When models are not near, scaling is key to fraction equivalency.

To **scale**, multiply the **numerator** and **denominator** by another whole.

The fraction's value won't change when this is done because you are multiplying by a fraction of one.

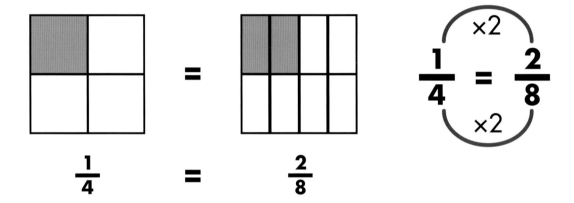

$$\frac{1}{4} = \frac{2}{8}$$

$$\frac{4}{4} = 1$$

In case you didn't know, fractions with matching numerators and denominators equal one whole.

When you are given a clue, use multiplication facts to find the missing equivalent numerator or denominator pair.

$$\frac{3}{4} = \frac{?}{8}$$

Time to find a missing numerator. Use the denominators shown as a clue. What number times 4 will equal 8?

$$\frac{3}{4} \overset{\times 2}{\underset{\times 2}{=}} \frac{6}{8}$$

Yes, it is true, multiplying by the whole, 2 over 2 will do!

$$\frac{3}{4} = \frac{6}{8}$$

Scale to find the missing equivalent fraction's part.

$$\frac{1}{2} = \frac{?}{10}$$

$$\frac{5}{6} = \frac{?}{18}$$

$$\frac{2}{3} = \frac{?}{9}$$

$$\frac{3}{4} = \frac{?}{16}$$

SIMPLIFY FRACTIONS

When simplifying fractions you need to find out
what greatest common factors are all about.

The greatest common factor is the largest **factor** that two or more
numbers share.

List the factors of each number, no matter how small
and pick the largest common factor of them all.

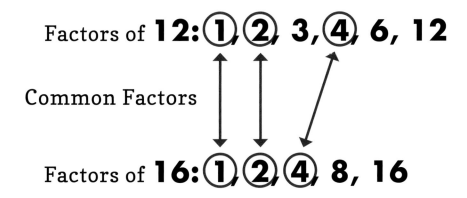

Factors of **12:** ①, ②, **3,** ④, **6, 12**

Common Factors

Factors of **16:** ①, ②, ④, **8, 16**

4 is the Greatest Common Factor of **12** and **16**

Simplest Form

Simplifying fractions reduces fractions to the **simplest form**. Just divide the numerator and denominator by their greatest common factor and you are through.

$$\frac{24}{32}$$

24 ⟵• Numerator

32 ⟵• Denominator

24: 1, 2, 3, 4, 6, ⑧ 12, 24
32: 1, 2, 4, ⑧ 16, 32

8 is the Greatest Common Factor of **24** and **32**

$$\frac{24 \div 8}{32 \div 8} = \frac{3}{4}$$

Divide by the greatest common factor to simplify each fraction.

$$\frac{9}{12}$$

$$\frac{8}{10}$$

$$\frac{12}{18}$$

$$\frac{5}{25}$$

COMPARE FRACTIONS

A number line with benchmarks is a useful tool
to compare fractions for me and you.

Comparing fractions starts by observing both their parts.

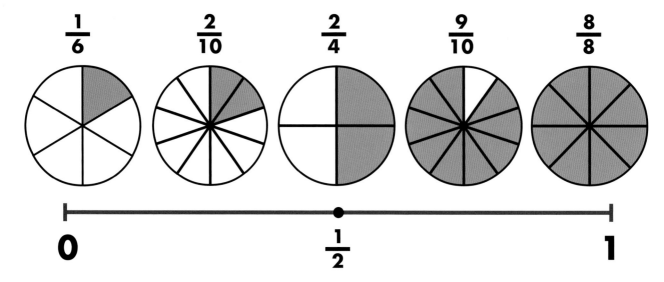

$$\frac{1}{6} \qquad \frac{2}{10} \qquad \frac{2}{4} \qquad \frac{9}{10} \qquad \frac{8}{8}$$

$$0 \qquad\qquad \frac{1}{2} \qquad\qquad 1$$

*When the numerator
and denominator are
far apart, the fraction is
considered very small,
almost nothing at all.*

*Uncovering one half is
very clear.*

*When the numerator
is close to half of the
denominator, one half
is near.*

*The closer the numerator
and denominator become,
the fraction is nearest the
whole number one.*

Answer true or false.

Use benchmark measures to check if each answer given is correct.

 $\dfrac{1}{2}$ $<$ $\dfrac{2}{3}$  $\dfrac{1}{5}$ $>$ $\dfrac{2}{4}$

$\dfrac{1}{3}$ $>$ $\dfrac{3}{4}$ $\dfrac{1}{4}$ $<$ $\dfrac{4}{5}$

$\dfrac{2}{4}$ $>$ $\dfrac{2}{6}$ $\dfrac{7}{8}$ $>$ $\dfrac{1}{2}$

$\dfrac{1}{2}$ $>$ $\dfrac{1}{4}$ $\dfrac{2}{4}$ $=$ $\dfrac{4}{8}$

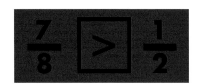

True
True
True
False

True
True
False
True

Answers:

15

To compare fractions with the same numerators, keep in mind that the denominator's job is to split the whole. As the denominator becomes larger, each part left for the numerator gets smaller and smaller.

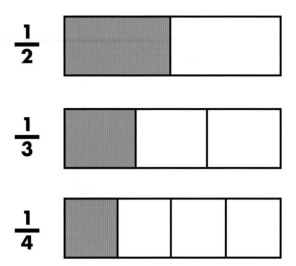

Comparing fractions with the same denominator is a breeze. The numerator controls how the fraction grows. Take a look and see why the numerator is key.

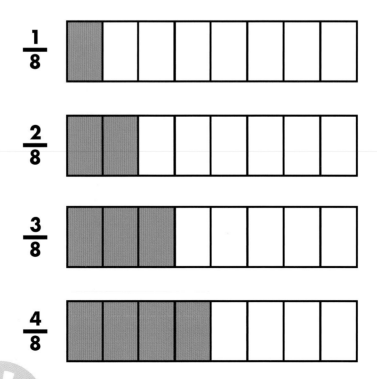

Answer true or false.
Use your knowledge of numerators and denominators to check if each answer given is correct.

Fractions with Like Numerators

$\frac{3}{5}$ ▢> $\frac{3}{10}$ $\frac{2}{3}$ ▢< $\frac{2}{9}$ $\frac{2}{5}$ ▢> $\frac{2}{6}$

$\frac{4}{4}$ ▢> $\frac{4}{8}$ $\frac{1}{8}$ ▢< $\frac{1}{3}$ $\frac{5}{15}$ ▢> $\frac{5}{10}$

Fractions with Like Denominators

$\frac{5}{8}$ ▢> $\frac{3}{8}$ $\frac{2}{5}$ ▢< $\frac{1}{5}$ $\frac{1}{8}$ ▢< $\frac{5}{8}$

$\frac{1}{6}$ ▢> $\frac{3}{6}$ $\frac{4}{10}$ ▢> $\frac{3}{10}$ $\frac{1}{4}$ ▢< $\frac{3}{4}$

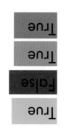
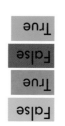
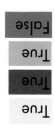
17

DECIMALS

As we already know, decimals show part of a whole.

They are always based on tens, so their denominators never have to be written.

Dividing a whole into ten equal parts is exactly what tenths are all about.

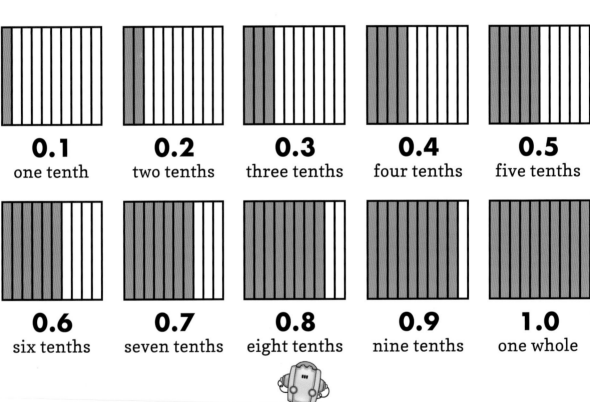

0.1	**0.2**	**0.3**	**0.4**	**0.5**
one tenth	two tenths	three tenths	four tenths	five tenths

0.6	**0.7**	**0.8**	**0.9**	**1.0**
six tenths	seven tenths	eight tenths	nine tenths	one whole

Check It Out!

The decimal point's job is to separate whole numbers from their decimal parts. For decimals less than one, place a zero in the one's place just for fun!

Now it is time to show how dividing a whole into 100 equal parts is exactly what hundredths decimals are all about.

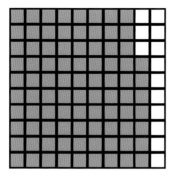

0.87
eighty-seven hundredths

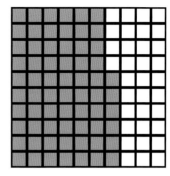

0.66
sixty-six hundredths

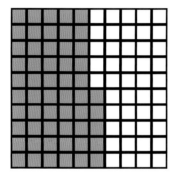

0.55
fifty-five hundredths

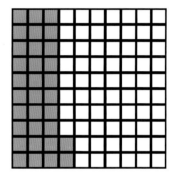

0.32
thirty-two hundredths

When a whole number appears before a decimal, say "and" for the decimal.
2.3 is read as "two and three tenths."
3.76 is read as "three and seventy-six hundredths."

Number lines are a perfect way to show how decimals and fractions relate.

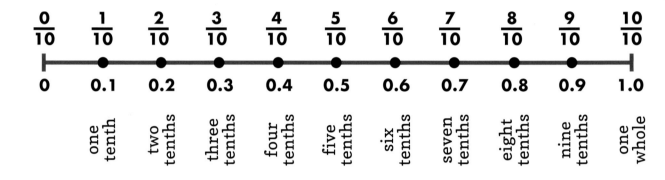

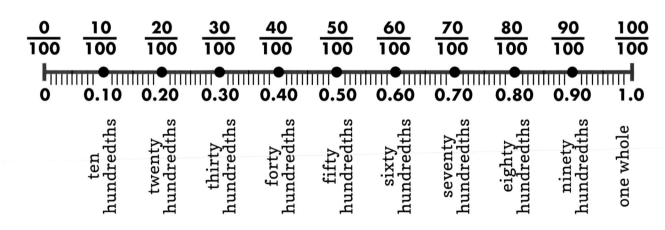

Name the fraction, decimal, and decimal number for each model or number line shown.

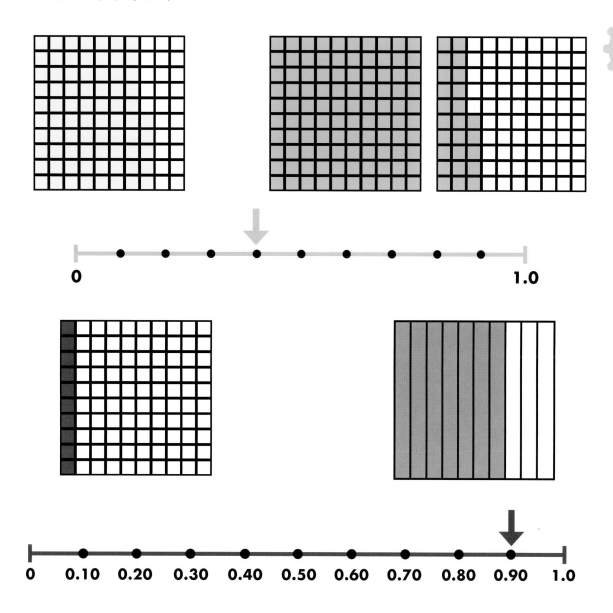

EQUIVALENT DECIMALS

Decimals are just like fractions and share equivalency.

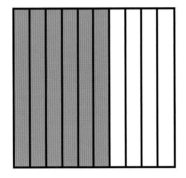

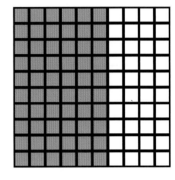

0.6 = **0.60**

six tenths   six hundredths

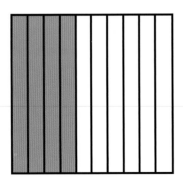

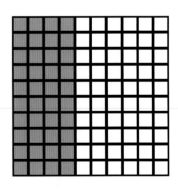

0.4 = **0.40**

four tenths   four hundredths

Number lines also help compare decimal equivalency.

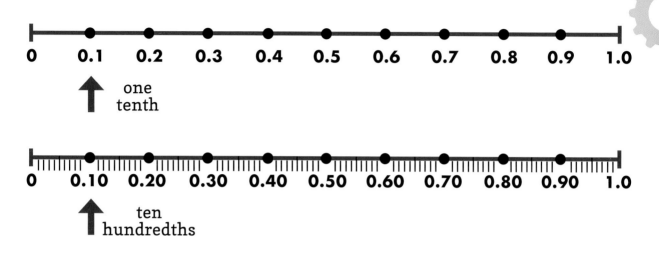

one tenth

ten hundredths

0.1 = 0.10

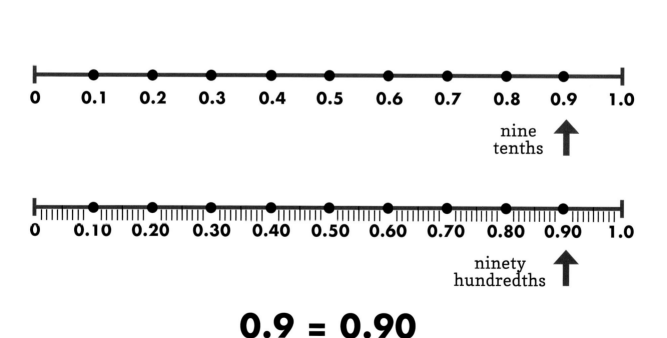

nine tenths

ninety hundredths

0.9 = 0.90

Scaling Decimals

Scaling decimal fractions using multiplication or division shows decimal equivalency.

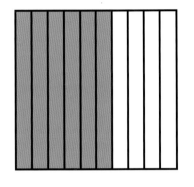 =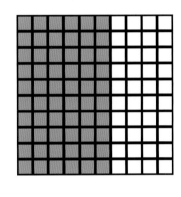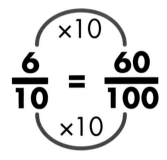

$$\frac{6}{10} = \frac{60}{100}$$

0.6

six tenths

0.60

six hundredths

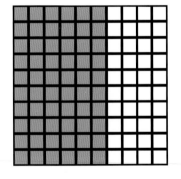 =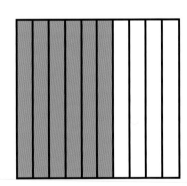

$$\frac{60}{100} = \frac{6}{10}$$

0.60

six hundredths

0.6

six tenths

Multiply to convert from tenths to hundredths.
Divide to convert from hundredths to tenths.

Scale to hundredths and show as a fraction and as a decimal.

0.3

$\dfrac{4}{10}$

$\dfrac{9}{10}$

0.1

Scale to tenths and show as fraction and as a decimal.

$\dfrac{80}{100}$

$\dfrac{50}{100}$

0.20

0.60

Compare Decimals

When comparing decimals, **annex** zeros as needed to make the place values match. Annexing zeros automatically scales decimals without changing the values.

Once the place values agree, you will soon see that comparing decimals is as easy as comparing whole numbers.

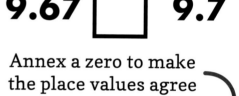

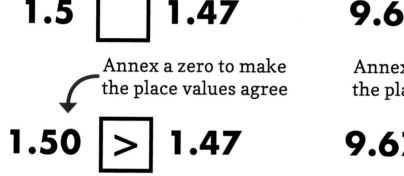

1.5 ☐ 1.47   9.67 ☐ 9.7

Annex a zero to make   Annex a zero to make
the place values agree   the place values agree

1.50 > 1.47   9.67 < 9.70

1.50 is greater than 1.47.   *9.70 is greater than 9.67.*
The ones are equal: *The nines are equal:*
0.50 is greater than 0.47.   *0.70 is greater than 0.67.*

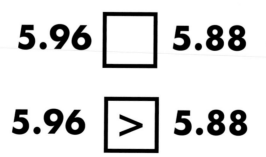

5.96 ☐ 5.88

5.96 > 5.88

5.96 is greater than 5.88.
The fives are equal:
0.96 is greater than 0.88.

Answer true or false.

Annex zeros as needed to check if each answer given is correct.

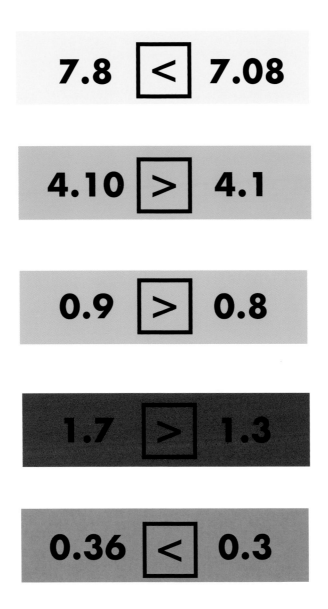

7.8 $<$ 7.08

4.10 $>$ 4.1

0.9 $>$ 0.8

1.7 $>$ 1.3

0.36 $<$ 0.3

Answers:

False
False
True
True
False

27

MONEY

When money comes out to play,
decimals to the hundredths are here to stay.

 =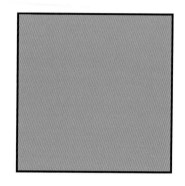

1 dollar = 1 whole

 =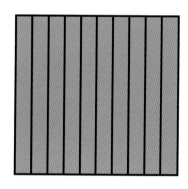

10 dimes = 1 dollar

 =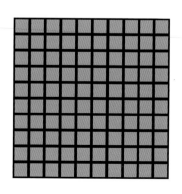

100 pennies = 1 dollar

Name the fraction and decimal for each amount of money shown.

GLOSSARY

annex (an-EKS): to place zeros at the beginning or end of a decimal benchmark

decimal (DESS-uh-muhl): a system of counting that is based on powers of ten

denominator (di-NOM-uh-nay-tor): the bottom number of a fraction that shows the number of equal parts of the whole

equivalent (i-KWIV-uh-luhnt): equal to

factor (fak-tur): the number or numbers that are multiplied

fraction (FRAK-shuhn): a number that is part of a group or part of a whole

numerator (NOO-muh-ray-tur): the top number in a fraction that tells how many parts of the denominator are taken

scale (SKALE): to multiply or divide a numerator and denominator of a fraction by the same value

simplest form (SIM-puhl-est FORM): when the only shared factor of the numerator and denominator in a fraction is one

INDEX

WEBSITES TO VISIT

www.mrnussbaum.com/fracdec

www.arcademicskillbuilders.com/games/puppy-chase/puppy-chase.html

www.sheppardsoftware.com/mathgames/decimals/DecimalModels10.htm

ABOUT THE AUTHOR

Lisa Arias is a math teacher who lives in Tampa, Florida with her husband and two children. Her out-of-the-box thinking and love for math guided her toward becoming an author. She enjoys playing board games and spending time with family and friends.

Meet The Author!
www.meetREMauthors.com

www.rourkeeducationalmedia.com

PHOTO CREDITS: Cover: © YuanDen, JDawnInk; Page 28: © Georgios Kollidas, Phillip Dyer, Peter Spiro

Edited by: Jill Sherman

Cover and Interior design by: Tara Raymo

Library of Congress PCN Data

Dandy Decimals: Add, Subtract, Multiply, and Divide / Lisa Arias
(Got Math!)
ISBN 978-1-62717-718-4 (hard cover)
ISBN 978-1-62717-840-2 (soft cover)
ISBN 978-1-62717-953-9 (e-Book)
Library of Congress Control Number: 2014935598

Printed in the United States of America, North Mankato, Minnesota

Also Available as: